THE LONG ROAD TO MARKET

From Isolation to Belonging

JULIA MILLER

Cover art by SelfPubBookCovers.com/RJWright

Interior art by D. Coonce

❀ Created with Vellum

This book is dedicated to the vendors of the 18th Street Farmer's Market.

FOREWORD

The journey into making Five Feline Farm a business has been like most journeys. Step by step. There is an end goal in mind, but the path is obscure. We keep moving forward, learning what to do next as each step is revealed. Our end goal is to provide a place of peace, a respite from the rush of the world.

As this venture has grown and developed, we have found it is a metaphor for our lives. We start small, unsure of our place in the world and what we will become. We grow into a community. A place where we stretch ourselves and find out what we are capable of, beyond what we thought we could be. We build connections.

Your goals and ours may be different, but the process to find belonging will be similar. Take each step as it comes, and above all enjoy the journey. Our road started lonely and bereft of direction. Now it is a vibrant journey, collecting friends like the flowers they are, offering rest and beauty.

Where does your road lead?

INTRODUCTION

"Who are these women of Five Feline Farm"?, you may ask.

Donna is the gardener and chief property planner. She excels in all things plant related, whether raising crops for market, tending the orchard she started from scratch or landscaping the Farm into a work of art. At this writing, Donna has a full time job teaching on line college classes.

Julia is the baker and the writer. She strives to turn the bounty that Donna raises into creative meals. She manages the website and Farm blog, occasionally guest posting on other blogs such as Mother Earth News. Julia has a full time job as a social worker.

As each of us near transition from our first career, we are building toward the future. We'll be too young to sit in rockers on the front porch day after day. This impending career change finds us building a small business on our farm. The business has grown from a hobby to a larger vision of providing a destination for others to join us in taking a moment to retreat into the peace of the country. In addition, building the business has secured us a place within our community, a place were we belong and are known.

As you read this book, you'll find much of it written from Julia's perspective so the use of "I" refers to me. We are both in this together, but I am the writer.

PREFACE

Five Feline Farm started as a concept in 2008 with the name. Initially it was a joke. To set up internet service and the new WiFi router, it had to have a name. There were five cats in residence and we are prone to drinking wine, so Five Feline Winery was the name applied to the router.

As we thought about our diverse interests and desire to become more self-sufficient, we morphed the name to a more encompassing title. Five Feline Farm was born. We even changed the router name to keep up with the times.

This is a small acreage in the midst of large farms. Surrounding us are corn and soybean fields, some wheat and hay. What can five and a half acres do? We researched hobby farms; small acreages that support families through a variety of avenues. We decided this plan could work for us. Five Feline Farm became an umbrella enterprise for all of our interests. The Farm sells vegetables, honey, wax-based products, educational materials, baked goods, jams, and is the publisher of our books. In 2017, the onsite store, Farm Fresh Mercantile opened. The Farmers Market became a natural extension of the farm concept—a place to start selling some of the excess we produce. It has turned into so much more.

In preparing crops and other items for market we rediscovered our heritage. My grandparents used to have an orchard and a few milk cows. They would sell fruit and milk to the local market. Donna's family, two generations ago, were also farmers.

We had no idea it would become this niche for us; a place where we belong in the community. We have developed relationships that bring us back to our roots where it has always been about connections.

PROLOGUE

P art of being in community and belonging to this thing greater than ourselves is sharing what we are learning to encourage others. There is little we won't try to accomplish on our own. In some tasks we have learned to ask for help, but those instances are few and far between. Typically this is after a failed attempt or two at accomplishing whatever is before us.

There is extreme satisfaction in being able to do for ourselves. Honestly, there is a good deal of impatience. When something crosses our minds, we want it done now. We can't wait to find someone and then wait for their time to do it. This approach has kept perfection from being the enemy of completion.

So what is the goal of this book?

It is to share a story of can-do. The tale of two women taking on a venture for which neither of us has training or experience. And it is more than that. In the telling, we hope to encourage others that it can be done. Do not let the things that you do not know how to do stand in the way of what you want to accomplish. Figure it out. Find a way to get the knowledge, support, materials, whatever it is that will get you the next step down the road. It is a story about finding community when you don't feel like you fit in.

Don't worry so much about seeing each step. It will come as it is needed. Just take the next step and the next and the one after that. If you wait to see the whole picture, you will wait forever and go nowhere.

Life is like that; you only get a glimpse of the next step. A good deal of faith is involved. You can choose what you believe and what faith means to you. To us, faith is an abiding trust in the infinite wisdom of God for our lives. We miss the mark often, but the deep knowledge in our souls that we are on the right path keeps us getting up every day and taking the next step.

The dream is worth it. Our community is worth it.

PART I
SEPARATE AND ALONE

CHAPTER 1

MOVING TO THE FARM

My farming story starts well before Five Feline Farm. I spent the first 12 years of my life in a country home and then a small village until I graduated from high school. Everyone I knew was connected to agriculture in some fashion. You might say farming is in my blood.

I've always loved being in the country. It brings me a sense of peace. When I say peace, I mean the kind that is deep within your soul, a knowing that all is right in the world. As a late teen headed off to college, I experienced a huge adjustment. Sirens and noises; busyness everywhere. I did appreciate the conveniences and I adapted. Eventually Donna and I bought a house and settled in, thinking this would be the place to stay forever. In this case, "forever" lasted 15 years. Then things began to change starting with my father's decline.

In the year before he died, Dad tore down a log cabin that had been in his family for generations. It was a monumental undertaking. My Dad never considered that he didn't have the right tools for a job he wanted to accomplish. He did with what he had. It wasn't always the right equipment or the really correct way of doing things, but he figured it out and made do.

So it was with the cabin. He devised a scheme for numbering the logs from bottom to top with the compass points serving as a reconstruction manual. Mom painted on all of the numbers. His dream was to use this cabin as a place to have the old things he collected in a museum; primitives, antiques and various items of unknown provenance. It wasn't just about collecting and hoarding but a place to share the knowledge and stories of these things he collected.

After disassembly, the logs were trucked 30 miles home and stacked; ready to build the museum of his dreams. It was not to be. His illness overtook his energy. He grew weaker and weaker. In his delirium he still gave instructions on how he planned to resurrect the cabin. We said goodbye to him in September 2000 and the logs languished in a stack. Weather began to take it's toll and the need to move them became critical.

I wanted these logs and to continue my father's dream. I had no idea how I would figure this out, but I am my father's daughter. I knew if the right place was available, I would find a way.

As the need to move the logs became more urgent, the search for land was on. There had to be a reasonably priced piece of land in the nearby area where a log cabin could be built without violating legal covenants. The land came through in a series of miracles, too long to recount here.

The cabin logs deteriorated over the next few years. I can still see the dream in my mind, but it was not to be. If I think too hard about it, the sadness takes over my heart, so I only concentrate on the things that are, not the lost things in the past. The cabin, although never resurrected, did get me to this land and where I am today. For that I am thankful.

Between 2002 and 2008, the responsibilities of maintaining two properties became overwhelming. Things had changed in the neighborhood in town and it was time to move. We had the land and decided to build a new home.

Building a new house is exciting and scary but we both loved every step of the process. Finally move in day arrived and we had most of our things in the new place. Who knew two people could accumulate this much stuff? Exhausted from the moving, I sank my weary body into bed the first night. I listened to coyotes singing in the field across the road. The sounds inside were different too. The house has it's own personality and settling sounds. The echoes are new. But it is quiet; no sirens or traffic. The night was still except for the occasional song of the coyote.

In the quiet I could feel my soul stretch and yawn. My very core settled into a new state of being. I breathed deeply of this new quietness and found myself at home; more truly and fully at home than I had been in twenty years. I didn't know I had missed the country life until that very moment. I had yearned for peace without acknowledging it was missing.

I still feel that now, any time I've been gone from this place for more than a day. When I return, I pull into the driveway and sigh a contented exhale of the busy world and inhale the peace of this place.

CHAPTER 2

ON OUR OWN

The seclusion of country life can be a curse as well as a blessing. We moved into the new home at the beginning of September, headed into the fall and then winter in a new place. The nearest neighbor is over a quarter mile away and someone we have never met. We are nine miles from town. It is not a great distance yet a long trek in the dark days of winter with snow piling up. We found our self-sufficiency skills would be tested in ways we were not expecting.

Slowly neighbors started dropping over to introduce themselves. They were surely curious about these two women who built such an enormous house. We struggled to remember who was who and how they all fit together. Many had been living in the area for a long time, some for all their lives. We were the new kids and didn't have relatives or connections here. Until we could figure out who to trust in the new neighborhood, we retreated into our own world, working feverishly to reclaim the land from years of neglect.

So, for the most part, we were on our own with some help from our families. All of our spare time was consumed with various projects around the farm to make our dream a reality. It was a relief to be away from the loudness of 20,000 people vying for their place in the world all at the same time. When we could, we planned our shopping to get as much as possible in one trip, making it commonplace to pick up necessities before or after work.

It was glorious to be removed from town life, yet after a period of time lonely. We yearned for connection and belonging to a community.

CHAPTER 3
MEETING A NEIGHBOR

B eing self-sufficient is a virtue and a vice.

We are both stubborn when it comes to doing all that we can for ourselves and not asking for help. A few times neighbors have taken pity on us and come to our aid. We are so grateful when that happens, but it is hard to admit we need help. Pride I suppose is what gets in our way, or maybe just a determination to demonstrate that we are capable.

For example, when we were first cleaning up the property, we demolished an old garage. It was falling in but was still surprisingly sturdy. We pulled down a number of supports and eventually the whole thing crashed down. It is different to accept help from family, and we did have help with the demolition. Then it was time for cleanup.

The plan was to drag the wood into a pit left from the old house basement and use that as a burn pit. It seemed like a reasonable idea and somewhat safer than burning where it fell near the road. It was only a few yards from the demolition pile to the burn pit, but still a mighty task.

We had hand tools; a rake, a saw, an ax and a wheelbarrow. We accepted it would take awhile to move and burn. Despite the hard work and hours of labor, we were willing to commit to this because it was ours to do. We had a plan and started to work it.

After only a few boards were moved, along came one of our new neighbors. He had stopped once before to introduce himself and give a brief history of the land. His family had owned this place two generations ago. He had fond memories of his grandparents and playing in the yard as a young child. Our vision of the property's future was much different than his memory of the past. We weren't sure what to think of him when he stopped this time; which was mostly embarrassment on our part. He looked around with a wonderment that did not disguise his amusement.

"Is this what you are using?" referring to the sorry pile of tools.

"This is what we have."

"I'll be right back."

Our befuddlement ended when he arrived in short order with his tractor and scoop. He was a true farm boy with a toy and a mission making short work of moving our pile of debris.

There were a few more awkward "song and dance" conversations over time before he acknowledged our right to the land and to make our own decisions, but we now had someone we could truly call a neighbor. Another step closer to being in community.

CHAPTER 4

PLANTING A GARDEN

C ountry folks garden. It is the lifestyle of the self-sufficient.
Now that we had ample land of our own, full of sunshine and possibilities, we were ready to put in a garden. In my vivid imagination, I could see row upon row of ripe vegetables, just waiting to be picked and processed for storage into the long dark winter. It would be easy to turn this sod, undisturbed for years with deep roots of grasses dug into the earth, into fertile, productive land. All we needed was a patch of soil clear of this grass. We selected the perfect place for the new garden plot. Of course at that time, there was no house, so we put the garden near the side of the property where we spent the most time.

Selecting the location of the garden was the easy part. We had no tools to till the earth and decided it was time to ask for help. We hired someone to till for us and the promise of freshly turned earth enthralled us.

Why would we have suspected that our perfect spot would end up to be full of sand?

The previous tenants had a pool there long ago, situated on a bed of level sand. It had grown over in grass by the time we found the property and a bit of soil inched across the top. Now that it was tilled, there was nothing to do but move forward. We planted anyway and were able to raise a few things; but not the bounty of my dreams.

Once we decided to build, the old garden plot was too far from the house to be useful. Who wants to trek all the way across the property to pick a tomato for supper? That fact, coupled with the knowledge the new site was in close proximity to the old barn and likely had cows running across it at one time made a perfect combination. I was convinced large bovines once trampled all over this area dropping what cows are known to do. After many years, this fertilizer from the cud chewing cow had seeped into the soil, enriching it for seasons to come. The new garden was bound to produce in line with my desires.

CHAPTER 5
MY GARDEN HISTORY

Both of us have farmers and gardeners in our family tree. There was a time when our families needed these gardens to supplement what they could afford at a grocery.

My grandma had a huge plot, laid out in lovely rows north to south. A berry patch and grape vines anchored one end. They had enough room to put in sweet corn and interspersed the whole thing with rows of flowers. I do remember her in her flowered house dress and apron, old worn shoes working her way through the rows with her hoe. I've seen her gather green beans up into her apron, using it in place of a bucket, then sitting in a lawn chair under the shade of the big tree near the back porch, snapping green beans for supper.

I loved when family would gather, especially my aunts and uncles who lived less than a mile away. Grandma didn't have air conditioning, so the shade tree and a cool breeze was the next best thing. They would all sit in lawn chairs in the shade during the hot afternoon and work through a bushel or two of green beans; their hands rhythmically keeping time with the lilt of their voices.

They discussed family events, community news, and most likely world news although I don't have a clear recollection of such discussion. I remember talk of where their grown children were and when they'd last heard from them.

I imagine their conversations in my memories.

"Sadie and her man went over to Greenville last week and found ground beef at that new store on the corner. They said it was good."

More snapping.

"Roxie isn't doing so good these days. I went over to see about her and she wouldn't hardly get up out of her chair. Ankles swollen so."

On it went until the last bean was gathered from the bottom of the basket, stripped of strings, snapped into perfect bite size pieces and dropped into the pot.

While the elders went about their gossip and work, I flitted in and out of the conversation. Sometimes sitting long enough to hear their conversation change to something more innocuous for younger ears and snap a few beans of my own. I watched Grandma's process as she barely took note of what her hands were doing. Millions of beans passed through those fingers under the shade tree.

I was never pushed away from the circle. I would go play from time to time, but also returned to the circle. I belonged here with the talk and the snapping where all were welcome.

Grandma would whisk the pot away to the stove; no doubt add some pan drippings from the breakfast bacon and put it on to cook, inviting all to stay for supper.

As I gather green beans into a pail from our own garden, I think about Grandma's hard working hands. I sit on my stoop and begin snapping. Donna and I now do this task together, talking about life and the news, occasionally pausing to listen to the birds. It is good conversation, but not the full circle of family and belonging. My memories are of a community, albeit all relatives, and I realized I crave the connections of friends and family perhaps more than the nutrition of the beans.

CHAPTER 6

DONNA'S FAMILY GARDEN

Ask Donna about her gardening history. Some of the stories go back another generation to include her great grandmother. She can describe in detail the experience.

Her eyes close as she accesses her memories. Sweet red cherry tomatoes are the first memory to surface. She speaks of walking through the garden with her Grandpa, picking the cherry tomatoes and popping the sun-warmed sweetness into her mouth. She recalls being maybe six or seven years old and the distinct impression she's sneaking a forbidden fruit. I picture her trailing a few steps behind an adult, slyly picking a tomato and eating it while watching for any sign she's been caught. Grandpa, of course knows exactly what she's up to and plays along, pretending not to notice. Years later she found out they knew all along and planted those just for her.

Flash back a few more years to her Great-Grandma Payne's garden. She worked there in her bonnet (Grandma, not Donna) daily to maintain the production, with Donna watching every task. A few weeds pulled one day, a few peppers harvested another, perhaps some thinning of new plants to encourage growth.

"What's that flower? Look at this bug! Grandma. Grandma, look!"

Grandma in her bonnet was ever patient, taking time to look at each new discovery and marvel along side this child. She must have been in her mid-70's at this time, still vibrant in her work ethic. She could watch a busy child while still sorting weed from food plant.

Donna's eyes fade to a distant time while she recalls her Grandma's garden. The connection to family and the land is evident as she recounts the free flowing conversation.

"How was school today, honey? Did you get to play some with your friends?"

Grandma always knew how to ask without prying and supported the emotions as well as the hunger of this young one.

Where has this time gone in our lives? Time spent together with family doing mundane chores that seemed like heaven to a child. Now we cram so many "must do" tasks into our allowed 68 hours each week. I feel in my soul something is missing.

CHAPTER 7
OUR OVERGROWN GARDEN

O ur farm is in East Central Illinois, not far from a large Amish settlement. Anyone who has been around the Amish, even for a short visit, can recall how their gardens look—not a weed to be seen; perfect rows of vegetables ready to feed their typically large families, and row after row of beautiful flowers. We drive through the country side just to ogle those works of perfection.

We started our housebuilding in late April of 2008; in fact, the basement was dug on the very last day of April that year. We had a general idea where the house was going to be and decided the year before to site the new vegetable garden near the house. We imagined a return to the way of potager gardens, a little kitchen garden ready to provide what I dreamed of as nearly instant meals with easy access to the kitchen.

So there it sat, the garden plot full of promise, next to the driveway bordering the new homesite. Mountains of clay piled around from the basement hole made it appear as if giant moles had invaded the land. Clay is not known to be exceptionally fertile but it can grow weeds. What appeared in our minds as picturesque rows of flowers and vegetables was instead a somewhat frightened group of tomatoes and peppers huddling together in the midst of a construction zone.

During the summer the house was built, other priorities overtook us in preparation for moving. There was packing, cleaning for the repeated open houses to sell the current house, and hour after hour of sorting years of accumulated jetsam and flotsam. We were still living nine miles away from this garden that held our food promises.

Not only was there packing and cleaning, but transplanting all the plant starts from the yard in town. We maintained a reference point to anchor ourselves in the process: we were either in town or on the farm. The new house never had a separate terminology for us in any way separated from the land. It was and is all collectively known as "the farm".

The new garden partially kept it's promise. The combination of newly tilled previously undisturbed sod with it's unreasonable weed seed load, and preparations to move kept us from doing much in the garden that summer. By late July, we decided it was a lost cause and stopped even trying. Weedy scattered vegetables was the forecast for the remaining months of harvest.

How does this involve the Amish?

Our contractor used Amish framers. They were here, climbing all over, building the house within full view of this messy garden. I imagined what they were thinking of us.

"Are these women serious about living in the country?"

"Do they have a clue what they are doing?"

I worried about whether they could be right. Did we belong here?

CHAPTER 8

LONELINESS

I am a self confessed homebody and a true introvert at heart. If I could, I would stay on the farm for days, maybe weeks at a time, leaving only for the absolute necessities. Sitting at home in my recliner is warm and comfortable. There is always social media to connect me to the outside world, or so I tell myself. It's easy although removed from actual reality. Technology today makes it easy to isolate oneself from human contact. We can go about our lives without interference. Even our families are scattered. In our busyness we forget about making true connections, looking each other in the eyes and experiencing a shared slice of life.

I go so far as to imagine myself in a cabin in the woods, far removed from civilization with only my books, a fire and a cat. Well, maybe two or three cats. Just a few solitary and quiet past-times to keep me from sheer madness. Of course that is neither a reality, nor is it a particularly healthy emotional state.

Due to work commitments, I'm not at home within my own four walls nearly as much as I would like. Being away from home so much for an introvert is exhausting. Even with this, I felt a pull to belong to something in the community that is greater than myself. There was a loneliness and a sense that something was missing. But, when you find yourself drained to the point you have little left to give and the prospect of responsibility to something else can be even more overwhelming, the doubts begin. Donna is more of an extrovert than I, but we both were hesitant. How do we break into an already established community where we really know no one? What are they going to think of these two women encroaching upon their territory? What if we don't fit in? The questions in my mind as we embarked on discovery of a community took up a position somewhere between relentless and nagging.

It's not as if we were total strangers to the community at large. We both know people around town, but as professionals in our respective disciplines, not as business owners and certainly not as market vendors. Even though it was only a few miles away we were now in a new neighborhood with a new way of living. We had developed only a passing knowledge of our neighbors.

There had to be another way.

CHAPTER 9

STARTING A BUSINESS

After a few years of cleaning up the property, building a house and moving in, the settledness allowed space for the question of "now what?" We had the distinct impression this land was given to us for something more than a place to call home although it was definitely that. There was something missing. It was hard to put words to, elusive of definition, but most definitely there in the background. Was it loneliness? Perhaps. But it was really more a sense of wanting to, or even needing to share this amazing blessing in some way. But how?

We had both belonged to a group before with a vision to provide a peaceful respite for others. Even after the group changed, we found that vision was still within us. Somehow this farm was to create a place of peace, a place of bounty that could be shared.

We talked through starting a bed and breakfast. We certainly have the space and breakfast is one of my favorite meals to cook. In visiting similar establishments, we enjoyed the hospitality, but at the end of the day we know having a bed and breakfast wasn't the answer. We are good hosts to a certain point, but we enjoy our privacy. That is not exactly a good combination for inviting guests into your home often enough for a viable business. Still we couldn't shake the feeling there must be a way to share this with others.

We tried a few tours. That was a lot of work for no real reward. That may sound haughty or prideful or greedy, which is not at all the sentiment behind it. We were looking for a business venture to sustain itself and support the vision.

As with everyone else on the planet, we grow older every day we are here. There is a time coming in our future when we'll be ready to leave the day jobs that have sustained us for all these years and venture out into something new. The dream of a farm business coupled with a measure of peaceful sharing became our motivation. At the same time we were pondering what to do, the garden began producing more abundance than we could possibly use. We gave to family and friends all they could handle plus a little extra when they turned their heads. An idea began to form. Could we sell the excess? Could we make that profitable enough to be worth scaling up the production? Who do we know that would buy? We have isolated ourselves and are not on the beaten path to anywhere. So many questions and no true answers.

We assessed the romance of a roadside stand. Even an honor system, where you put out a can and a table of produce, then bingo. The place takes care of itself.

That is a lovely dream or vision if you live on a well travelled road to somewhere. But we feared that, anyone well traveling this road has their own garden. We are in the midst of one of those places where people mostly lock their car doors to keep others from leaving zucchini in the seat. We see it up and down the road.

We discovered a fairly recently formed Farmer's Market in town and as we pursued options to become involved, we wanted to offer different things than the primary focus of produce. We do have produce but not on the scale required to make a living. We had ideas for a wide variety of other products. Would these fit in with this market? There was no way to know unless we took the step of signing up and finding out.

PART II
FINDING THE MARKET

CHAPTER 10
THE DRAW OF A MARKET

Something about the atmosphere of a market draws me in. Perhaps a good part of it is visual; row after row of gleaming fruits, vegetables and other goods. The selection is overwhelming and I immediately think of all the delightful things I can cook. As I shop, my mind is planning meals for these raw ingredients. Sometimes it is just one ingredient that I will add to an already planned meal, say minced peppers in scrambled eggs. Other times, I find green beans to slow cook with new potatoes that bring back memories of growing up with this down-home simple meal. When the sweet corn is abundant, I'll make a meal out of just that.

I'm not particularly fond of the crowds, but I accept that is part of it. Jostling for position to get near the front of the booth is not my idea of camaraderie. I like calm and order. I'm willing to wait my turn but I'm also on a mission. There is no time to wait for the old lady in the funny hat and big basket to squeeze every tomato debating about the freshness. She aggravates me when she sucks her teeth and disparages the price.

"Come on lady. I have got to get my stuff and get to work. He isn't trying to steal your last dollar. Make a decision and move on."

Thankfully my social skills are engaged enough to keep these thoughts to myself.

I'm also seeking the best tomato for what I have in mind to make so I feel a bit of remorse at my crankiness. But what do they expect? I gave up a cup of coffee to be here. I thrill to find something unusual from time to time. A different colored pepper perhaps or a new variety of potato. Something I can experiment with and create a new dish.

I watch the vendors in their appointed stalls, vying for the attention of customers through their product placement and displays. They periodically adjust their product so the best side is forward. They answer questions about uses, fragrance and make recommendations of the best choices for the intended use. You can spot the customer and vendor relationships. The first time customers who flit from station to station eyeing the produce with minimal eye contact to the vendor. The established relationships where customer and vendor discuss more than the sack of peas exchanging owners. I bask in the emotional comfort of the small town feel.

I also like to visit markets far from home. It's great fun to see ones with access to different fresh foods not typically available in landlocked Illinois. There is still a sense of community I feel in these places. Yes, it's bigger and easier to move in and out of the crowds in anonymity. You could probably commit a crime in some of these large venues with a decent chance of escape. I'll save that for a fiction novel. There are still the obvious regulars. Customers and vendors who have each been in their regular places week after week for years on end. No doubt they find comfort and ease in the dependable nature of those interactions.

One such market is Pike Place Market in Seattle. I could spend hours and days exploring every stall in this market. It has the stability of longevity. It is easy to spot vendors who are in the same stall they've been in for eternity. They cater to a population that demands freshness and quality. Of course the fish market there is world-renowned. It's encouraging to see that kind of success. The market has restaurants too with combinations of fresh ingredients from nearby vendors; everything from street food to high cuisine. All of this and a relaxed atmosphere.

The Reading Terminal Market in Philadelphia has that same feel. Vendors with cheeses and meats, drinks and pastries. The local Amish come from the surrounding countryside with their fresh items. These are true artisans offering something for everyone.

Let's not forget Soulard in St. Louis which also has that old world market ambiance. I envy those who live close enough to walk or ride a bike to fill their reusable canvas bag with a few days of groceries. I imagine that if I lived in a city, I would want to be near enough to just such a market that I could shop every couple of days. I would plan just a meal or two in advance to eat from local or world wide cuisines. All this with ingredients found just around the corner.

CHAPTER 11
SHOPPING THE MARKET

Before there was an 18th Street Farmer's Market in Charleston and before we moved to the farm, there was the Wednesday Market on the Square. I should say there still is; the Wednesday Market continues but it predated our involvement with the Saturday Market.

We lived about a mile across town in those days and the Wednesday market started at 7:00AM. My nature is not that of an early riser; I love to stay in bed with the covers pulled up tightly, eyes shut against the world. It takes great effort to finally will my body to throw back the covers and start the day. My eyes don't necessarily open until I hit the kitchen and a cup of coffee. Even if my eyes have opened, my brain does not leave the warmth of slumber until caffeine washes the synapses. Much the same way our cats refuse to acknowledge the outside world until something enticing enough commands their attention, I delay the inevitable. For them, it is the opening of a food can. For me, it is the promising aroma of coffee and caffeine diffusing through my veins.

The promise of fresh vegetables for the week however, could also pull me out of bed. In a nod to the health of shopping for these fresh colorful foodstuffs, I even rode my bike. The early morning rides downtown, empty backpack waiting to be filled, felt good. I rode around the square, eyeing each vendor's wares, subconsciously noting how they displayed what they had to offer. After careful study during the first pass, I returned to my chosen vendors, stuffed my purchases into my backpack and peddled off quite pleased with myself.

I adored the variety, the freshness and the camaraderie among the vendors. I appreciated their life of connection with their land, their produce and their neighbors, sharing that abundance with those of us in town without the space to provide such freshness for ourselves. I hated for the season to end; forced back to frozen, canned and shipped out of season produce at the local grocery. But more than just consuming the vegetables, I wanted to belong to that life.

CHAPTER 12

THE 18TH STREET MARKET

W e are building that same feel right here in Charleston, Illinois.
The 18th Street Farmer's Market doesn't have the daily
offering nor the permanent stability of indoor booths where vendors
work year round. Our market maxes out the space at 25 vendors or so
and we are limited by health regulations on some items.

But on Saturday mornings, from mid-May through September, the
asphalt parking lot is transformed into a market. Tables and tents
appear from the beds of pickup trucks, music plays in the background
of chatter between customers and vendors. Out of nowhere, the city
feel of a longstanding market has arrived.

Vendors work shoulder to shoulder, keeping fellowship through the
slow times. Traffic is diverted around the market space so children and
adults can roam free between booths. Customers make the rounds,
planning their purchases and menus simultaneously as they survey the
weekly offering. On the second pass, they make their selections,
choosing what will get them if not through the week, at least through
the next few days.

A few hours later, it is all gone. No evidence that a market once
stood between the light poles and parking lines. But echoes of conver-

sation remain with me. Discussions about tomatoes and sweet corn, honey and scones; talk of the week past and the week coming. New customers, seasoned vendors and repeat shoppers have all appeared in the same place for the same purpose.

The city has come to the small town.

CHAPTER 13
PREPARING FOR MARKET

I love to bake. Really it is more than that; I love to feed people. The ability to sell something I make was a bonus for me at the market. There had been changes in the Illinois Cottage Food laws which created a space where I could bring to market a bit of my passion for baking.

The challenge became what to sell. There are still limits on what can be sold from a home kitchen at the Farmer's Market. I had no idea where to begin, but I knew there were others who had done this so it must be possible. I started researching and found the list of rules, but all were doable. As long as I was selling a "non-hazardous" baked good with the proper permits, I could make this a reality. Then came the big decision on exactly what would be my specialty.

I used to make cinnamon rolls for friends and family at Christmas time. While I loved doing that, the more I tried to make, the more the quality suffered. Of course, everyone still raved about them, but I knew it wasn't the same. So eventually I tapered off with that and looked for something new. In my quest for something satisfying, I transitioned to making scones. Scones are a quick bread, easy to make and as the style suggests, quick to bake. Scones also lend themselves to a level of pre-preparation that works well for this venture. The dry ingredients can be measured and mixed in advance, then the final preparation goes quickly.

Whether you say "scohnes" or "scahnes" on Saturday morning, the kitchen at Five Feline Farm transforms into a bakery and I am in a happy place.

CHAPTER 14
WORKING WITH THE RULES

Naturally there are detailed requirements in the cottage food laws, but we were able to get all of the permits the week before the market opened for the season. It was in the nick of time, but we made it. Despite our personal feelings about the sensibility of the laws, at this time, it is the law and until it is changed, we will follow it.

The local health department is charged with ensuring the Farmer's Market complies with state law. When you are selling produce, this is fairly straightforward: keep the produce in it's whole state with minimal trimming or rinsing. Displays and food products must be off the ground. Consumers should expect to clean and wash produce before use.

Baked goods are another matter. There was a time in Illinois when baked goods were strictly prohibited at Farmer's Markets. Even though this is a state law, it is up to the local health department to enforce the law. Our county has a reputation for being one of the most strict in the area. When selling in other locations we were told that if we can meet the requirements in our home county, we'll be fine in others. Although as a vendor I sometimes chafe against the rigidity, as a consumer I appreciate the attention to detail.

The best advice we can give is to work with and not against the health department. Start with research on the rules, then talk to someone at the health department. Find out what they are looking for, what forms they need and get their advice along the way. Even though there may be many steps, keep in mind the shared goal is for no one to have a bad experience consuming your home-made products.

The next piece of advice is to start planning well in advance. Our Market starts in mid-May, so we start preparations in January. The first step to a Cottage Food permit is a Food Service Sanitation Manager (FSSM) certification.

The FSSM involved taking a course online at the local community college and then testing. It is more difficult than you think and really makes you look at other food operations differently. I didn't eat out much while taking that class. Eight weeks later, task complete.

Then I had to register my national test score with the State of Illinois. This took a few weeks for the State to decide they would link up my money with my registration. As more time passed and the start of the Market was looming I began to get a bit nervous. The application for my county permit was complete except for that state license.

While waiting for my state application to crawl through the process, I took my application to the health department for a review. They were more than accommodating and truly gave the impression they wanted me to succeed. Developing this relationship early on was most valuable. The sanitarian working with me pointed out some areas I should consider and helped refine my menu.

Finally, the state certification arrived and I turned in my application. The next part went quickly and, with only a clarifying question later, I had my county Cottage Food permit for the year. It was the Wednesday before the Market started on Saturday. I made it.

As I've looked back on this time of meeting what felt like an unreasonable number of steps and certifications, I realize it did more for me than just acknowledge that I can follow rules. Our vendor booth has been inspected during markets and always passes without a problem. We work hard to ensure that we are in full compliance with the law as not only a mark of respect for the duties of the health department sanitarians, but also as responsible community members.

CHAPTER 15
FRIDAY NIGHT PREPARATIONS

The first Friday night was nerve wracking. I kept trying to swallow the knot in my throat placed there by fear of the unknown. Questions crept into my brain despite my best attempts to plug up the entry.

"What if we look dumb?"

"What if our prices are too high? Or too low?"

"We can always adjust."

"There is a first time for everything", I keep telling myself.

My inability to sleep amplified my anxiety. I knew it was irrational and not on the same plane as say, a bear attack, but it was a real lump in my throat.

The average Friday during market season looks something like this:

Donna picks and packages produce starting in the early morning and for as long as it takes. While she's there she takes time to weed the lettuce beds while the shade cloth is pulled back. Each type of vegetable is hand-picked, packaged and stored in the refrigerator if necessary. One after another each crop is picked, packaged and stored until everything is ready to go.

Whatever can be pre-loaded in the truck is loaded. We have a system for loading and unloading. Everything is stored together in an easily accessible place so the loading time is as efficient as possible. We have managed to either obtain or build things that will store and load easily. Our signage folds up, totes contain non-perishable products and display parts. We have folding tables and the awning folds up into it's own bag.

While all the outdoor preparations are occurring, inside as much advance preparation as possible for the baking is done on Friday. We have tried offering special baked goods that could be done on Friday. For example, in strawberry season we took shortcakes. A few weeks later we offered biscotti to meet several customer requests. Our standby however, is scones. We started with three flavors, cherry walnut, cinnamon chip and chocolate chip. This has expanded into our current run of six flavors each week. There has been a learning curve with how to produce these as quickly as possible while maintaining the quality we want to provide.

We are really at maximum capacity for scone production on a Saturday morning. I have noted this several times since we began this adventure, but truly we can do no more. The Friday preparation makes Saturday morning go much quicker and maximizes our time available for cooking. We are now limited only by the oven capacity and our time.

Donna often begins her preparations earlier in the week, making balms and surveying what produce will be ready. She plans the order of harvest; greens and tender lettuces in season are picked early in the morning before the heat of the day has a chance to wilt them. Potatoes and carrots may be done later in the day. She also works the advertising circuit of social media posting not only the scone flavors, but the full range of available produce. She excels at maintaining customer involvement and interest.

Friday also finds us managing any last minute price research. Donna compiles the product and price list for our records then finalizes the market sign. It is a balancing act between offering new things and what we know will sell. We try to branch out but also stay with some of our standbys, like the scones and cat toys.

Friday nights are different for us now. Most people relax at the end of the work week. Friday is their night to go out to eat, take in a movie, see a concert, maybe just a simple shopping trip to get groceries. Of course, we are not most people.

Instead of going out, it is an evening to spend at home. We are preparing for market. If things have gone well for us during the week, we do have a moment to wind down, relax and get to bed early.

If we are running behind, I bring home something quick for supper and we eat while finishing up the market prep. We would rather not do that in keeping with our "eating local and fresh" goal. Home cooked is best because we know what is in it, how it was treated and prepared.

So Friday nights are not always peaceful. The days are long; preparations are demanding. It takes a lot for just two people to maintain this. We both have high standards when it comes to presenting our products and making a go of this business. Keep in mind that we are both working full time outside of the farm and have the usual chores every other household does. Other than major repairs we do it all ourselves.

Is that crazy? Maybe.

Self-sufficient? Definitely wherever possible.

The best Friday night has a minimum of final preparations. The scone bags are labeled and ingredients measured. The truck is loaded. We have a moment to sit on the deck listening to the whirr and twitter of the hummingbirds as they dive and spat with each other, vying for the optimal perch to get a drink. They fill up with sustenance for their flight ahead, even if that flight is just across the yard to check out the gladiolus.

Early to bed on Friday night. The morning will arrive early. After that first morning making scones and the need to bake as many as possible, I decided 3:30 AM was a good start time. Really, who does that? Friday for usual people is a fine night to stay up late with no Saturday obligations. We are not usual people. A bedtime of 9:00 PM or so gives me enough sleep to be able to jump up and be ready to go. Typically there is time for a nap in the afternoon. By Sunday, my sleep cycle is back to normal.

CHAPTER 16

OUR FIRST FARMER'S MARKET

It was finally time for our first market. We had practiced briefly setting up in our driveway the day before the market started. Like so many other things, we found ourselves rushing around at the last minute. In this, the two of us are not so very alike. In most things we communicate quite well, but planning finds us miles apart. And the most baffling part is that it is inconsistent which direction we each will take. In this moment of practicing our set up, I had some ideas in my head about it, but failed to share. Donna was ready weeks before to practice.

I am a direction follower. I believe in opening the directions, locating all of the parts, checking them off the list, laying them out in order of use, then proceeding to assess if the directions are correct. Donna is more one to experiment; just start plunging ahead and don't waste time on unnecessary steps. A little pounding with a hammer will make most parts fit together.

Thankfully, awnings and table arrangements are not quite so complicated. Still, I should have listened and made time to practice setting up. That would have given the nervous little butterflies less room to maneuver in my intestines.

We rolled onto the asphalt dance floor early with the wallflower jitters. It's never good to be the first to arrive. Questions flooded my brain overpowering my fragile synapses. How do we know where to go? Where do we stand? How long will it take to get a customer? Can I fade into the sidelines?

We didn't have a clue how this was going to go at our first market. We did as much as possible over the preceding months to plan, but the day had arrived. Had we prepared enough? The Junior High dance butterflies threatened to expose themselves, crawling right up my esophagus. Still there were more questions than answers.

There were offers to help as we set up our tent.

"No, thank you. We can do it."

Even if I couldn't banish the fluttering, I could keep it invisible from others.

Ok, so they were just being kind, and in retrospect the help would have been nice. At that moment, I didn't understand how the pressure of the awning against the leg would impact how well it goes up and down. I learned the painful way to expand the tent before raising the legs. That simple step of picking it up a little to take the pressure off those damned little buttons keeps you from pinching your fingers when you push them. Now I know two things. First, how to easily manipulate awning legs. Second, and more importantly: allow others to give their advice. In the end you can take it or leave it, but if you don't even listen, you might experience unnecessary pain.

We spread out our wares on small tables and I judged it a paltry offering. Looking around we found another vendor with baked goods, yet another with plant starts. The queasiness was starting to return as I assessed there is nothing special about us outside of my excitement. Of course I held it in to keep the calm exterior face forward. Being the new kids we were sure no one would dance with us.

Determined to make the best of it, we finished our set up and surreptitiously checked prices around us. Our pricing was spot on. One butterfly conquered. The research into the University of Illinois Extension price lists had paid off. But look at what all of the other vendors brought to market.

We had on the same dress as every other girl at the dance. Not literally of course, but other than a few random items (no one else brought cat toys) we had many of the same things as everyone else. It was embarrassing. Time to call in all the butterflies in the county to roost in my gut.

Nervously we waited for our first customer. And waited. We watched the other vendors and their established relationships begin to make sales.

Of course the belle of the party had his own large trailer with raised concession windows. He earned a premium spot. Butterflies now added green envy to their internal repertoire.

After what felt like hours but in reality was a few minutes someone strolled up. We put on our best engaging faces and greeted this potential buyer. Was there anything at all on our table she might want? No.

Well "Thank you for stopping by" anyway.

How about this person? She looks ready to buy.

Yes! We scored a customer. Finally, someone wanted to dance with us. A quick spin around the tables and a sale was made. Then another and another. We nearly sold out of my assessed paltry offering we took to the first market. In just that first day it was obvious we could expand and grow. Elation ruled the afternoon.

The thrill of assessing our dance card was palpable. We hoped for $100. That small amount would give us the encouragement to go on, the possibility that we could manage this beginning business. It would be worth it. Any little bit of profit to prove we were entrepreneurs and ready to enter the dance floor every Saturday.

Would it be time to celebrate?

CHAPTER 17
FIRST MARKET SUCCESS

That first day was truly exhilarating yet scary as a new small business owner. We had never been vendors at a Farmer's Market before or anywhere else for that matter. We had some history as presenters at conferences, but never as a bonafide vendor. This was not even a familiar market to us; we had visited a couple of times the year before so had only a rudimentary picture in mind of what to expect. Coming back home that first Saturday, I was anxious to know how the day turned out financially. Of course we had to unpack the truck first and put away a few things. We also needed something for lunch. I was starved as noted by my insistent rumbling belly. The cash box would have to wait.

It sat on the table with it's mysterious treasures. After ensuring all of the necessary chores were complete, eagerly I opened it and started counting. Would we meet our $100 goal? Anything close to that would be successful in our opinion. I didn't even know if that was a good target, but it seemed like a reasonable place to start. I was simultaneously excited, nervous and a bit embarrassed that this was important. Yet it was an indicator of whether or not this venture was worth the time and effort. It is not an easy thing to pack up week after week and stand on asphalt, waiting for someone to be interested enough to part with some cash.

I pulled the bills out of the cashbox and spread them on the counter. It looked like a lot. The cash box had started the day with $100 to make change. It had only taken an hour to discover that $100 in small bills was not enough change on hand to meet the need. I watched the dollar bills disappear.

"Does no one carry dollar bills anymore?"

"Seriously, another twenty? What is it with these people?"

Muttering to myself did not change the fact that I needed to make a run to the bank. It was distracting to manage the ongoing dialogue in my mind, plan for a break in the action, decide where the nearest bank is, how much to get and how fast I could get back.

You would think one week of running short on change would encourage me to plan better the following week. Not so. At least three consecutive weeks, I made a run for change until I finally figured out how to balance that financial task.

Back to counting money.

It was unbelievable. I counted twice to be sure. I felt giddy.

$215.

Did I count that right? I checked and double checked before announcing to the house. Then Donna counted. Yes! It was correct. We made more than double our expectations on the first day. We sold all of our baked goods and all of our produce.

So now what? Time to find a way to add more product to our offering to sustain this success and grow.

I rode that high the rest of the weekend. Exhilarating doesn't capture the full emotion. We were vendors and Five Feline Farm was in business.

CHAPTER 18
WEEK TWO

We survived the first dance of the butterflies. The next Saturday was supposed to be effortless; after all, we are experienced entrepreneurs now. It wasn't exactly effortless, but it was easier the second week. We pulled in five minutes ahead of the scheduled set up time. We now knew the drill and could go directly to our spot. Unloading the truck was quicker and soon we were awaiting our first customer of the day.

The butterflies of last week quickly gave way to the hackles of defensiveness. One of the other vendors came over to check our prices. He wasn't even discrete about it.

I smiled sweetly while my brain screamed "get back to your own tent". We both had essentially the same wild flowers. Black eyed Susan's, Yarrow, Queen Anne's Lace, Coneflower; beautiful flowers looking like they would grace anyone's table.

Ours were small arrangements designed for the customer to take home and put in their own vase. The neighbor had a few more flowers and included a mason jar and a ribbon. He blatantly checked our arrangements and prices. The hackles were going to start showing through my shirt if he didn't move on quickly. Then it came out. He thought we were charging significantly more than he was. On closer exam, we figured out our sign had a bump in it that made it appear we were charging more than we actually were. That in addition to the different size of the arrangements made our respective prices make sense. The end result was that he felt better about their pricing and we got a chance to clarify our sign.

As much as we felt assessed by others, we also sized up the competition and found areas of our operation to improve. Knowing the week would fly by, we had to hustle to make those improvements.

One thing immediately apparent was that scones were a big hit. This was a clear win and an item that could quickly be scaled up. Now, by "scaled up", I mean getting up earlier and baking more. Yes, this could work but what if we could also offer other baked goods? My brain exploded with options. I could do pies and cookies; what about breads and cupcakes? I experimented with new flavors of scones and making double batches. Finally my better sense kicked in and I thought about what could realistically be done in the time available. I settled on occasional cookies or biscotti on Fridays and worked up to six double batches of scones on Saturday morning.

Since this was our first attempt at a Farmer's Market, we weren't entirely sure how to set up and arrange our tables and items. Before the season we did some research about table set up and displays. We then adapted some of those setups to our products and what works best for us. We started with a small pop up awning and a couple of tables. We knew to cover the tables with tablecloths, and when it was raining, pull in a little closer so all of our products were under cover. Customers could come in out of the rain a bit when needed.

The first Saturday found us a bit lacking in how we displayed our items. It is hard to know how to set everything up until you've done it a few times. We made minor changes where possible by the second week, but until the Farm started producing significant income, we would have to continue on in our hand-me-downs. We were testing the waters and not going to invest a lot of cash if this wasn't going anywhere.

We tend to do a lot of repurposing, partly because it thrills me and partly from necessity. For the scones, I scavenged racks from an old greenhouse plus some old 2x2's and screwed it all together into a collapsible display rack. It sounds cooler than it actually was. For the produce displays, old brood boxes from defunct beehives were cleaned up, bottoms added and a fresh coat of paint slapped on the sides. A quick fabric lining and we had display boxes. We used a couple of top feeders from the hives because they are watertight to hold ice and ice packs to keep the lettuce and other fragile items cool. The sun and heat beating down on asphalt is not kind to fragile produce. Even though we liked the theme of using parts from beehives in our display, they are heavy and awkward to load and unload each week.

CHAPTER 19

IMPROVEMENTS

After a few weeks, we decided we needed a better sign. It was time to step up yet another part of the game. As always I looked around to see what could be salvaged into a sign. I had an idea of what I wanted; a sandwich style board painted with chalkboard paint. The items and prices could be changed weekly with updates. A few boards lying around were quickly ripped to make 2x2 lumber and a smooth piece of plywood painted with chalk board paint. Voila. A chalkboard sandwich board.

All was well and good until it hit the ground a few times in gale force winds. Ok, maybe not gale force, but most definitely strong enough to bring a sign crashing to the pavement startling all within several feet. More than one person had their finger pinched trying to grab the sign and keep it from toppling over. Even after shelling out some hard earned cash for a fancy new dry erase board, the wind has her way with it.

There were some things however that were just required like food safe containers for transporting baked goods. There was something about going to the commercial kitchen supply store that made this feel real. Rows of gleaming stainless steel beckoned me to run my hands over the smooth metal. It felt fresh and clean and full of promise. I flashed back to movies where chefs purchase beautiful equipment for their restaurant or food truck. I want to do that but on a more frugal budget. We made do for a while with things such as a used large cooler to haul the fragile produce in the back of the truck, the home-made display racks, our repurposed tables and the all important lawn chairs. I do wonder now why we even bother to pack lawn chairs. We never sit. Occasionally visitors to our stand sit while they talk to us, but somehow we never have time. Plus, sitting is not as inviting as standing to greet customers and to engage them as friends.

Each week we have continued to make adjustments in how we do things. It is never the same twice, although it is getting closer. Over time we have added equipment and changed out displays as our operation grows. Finally, every thing we need is stored together in totes and baskets so we can load and unload quickly.

CHAPTER 20

AWNINGS IN THE WIND

Most Farmer's Market vendors in these outdoor venues carry collapsible awnings that are erected and taken down each time. These are mobile markets taking over vacant lots or empty parking areas so temporary structures are the norm. A few vendors have a truck or trailer, but by and large tent city appears any time the Farmer's Market is in session.

Every one of these blasted awnings have a little bit different mechanism. There are buttons and rails and fabric. Throw in a lever or two and you have an almost endless array of systems to manipulate an awning. Some of them can be cantankerous to set up and each has it's own pinch points. Add a bit of wind, or even the merest breeze when you are stretching out your awning and you will feel like you are holding on to a larger than life kite. I imagine this is what it must feel like to handle a balloon in the Macy's Thanksgiving parade. Occasionally a gremlin wedges the parts together and it is all I can do to keep from growling obscenities.

Awnings on asphalt. That's how we roll. No stakes to firmly plant our awnings to the ground. There is an art to keeping an awning stable on asphalt in wind. Imagine spindly legs suspending a windsail eight feet in the air. Given there is no way to pin the legs to the ground, we all have adapted various styles of weights. Look around and you will find all kinds of options from filled water jugs to weights designed to be filled with sand and wrapped around the legs. Some use discs that are full of sand and slide onto the legs. A few very creative and crafty folks have designed their own weights ranging from milk jugs filled with concrete or sand to lengths of PVC pipe filled with concrete and old iron window weights hung from the corners. We started with jugs of kitty litter. Really, what else would you expect from Five Feline Farm? We have now graduated to four five-pound round disks to weight the legs. These provide some anchoring and support but are not foolproof.

We assume the vendor stance. We all do it. Hanging onto the leg of our awning or maybe the bottom rail of the top. It looks like the vendor has been suspended there and with only a small price tag, could actually be for sale. It is just our need to hold on before everything takes flight. Despite our combined best efforts, I have witnessed all of these methods fail in a good strong wind.

One particular summer day seemed perfectly fine as we set up. The breeze picked up, but then tapered off again. Everything was running smoothly. All of a sudden, from nowhere a gust tore through the market. It lifted our weighted awning, toppling it into our tables and knocking over the whole she-bang. In the process of trying to catch everything, I was whacked in the head by an aluminum leg. We scurried to get our products back in order with help from neighbor vendors as well as a couple of customers. We also helped our neighbors as best we could. Everyone was back in business within short order, although I sustained a knot on the head. Another vendor fared worse with a broken awning leg. After a startled moment all was stabilized and we continued with sales.

Dealing with the weather is part of how this works. You get sun, rain, wind, cold and heat. There are ways to accommodate and make the best of each, but it still requires fortitude to manage.

We have observed an interesting phenomenon at this Farmer's Market. Vendors in competition with each other to sell their goods are at the same time quite helpful to their competitors. There is a common understanding that what helps one, helps us all. We are blessed to have both witnessed and participated in this common good. Not only do we help each other hold awnings in the wind, but from time to time there has been the loan of a bungee or help taking down and putting up tables.

Help also comes in the form of advice. Vendors share information about taking credit card payments, which of the scanners they feel is best for their business and how to gain the ability to accept Farmer's Market coupons issued by the state. It might be something about the shared goals to sell our wares, or maybe it is just a gathering of good people.

As we experience help from others, we also try to help our neighbors when we can. New vendors are often taken by surprise when their competition helps set up their awning. I know they are watching out of the corner of their eyes at the veteran vendors while trying to set up and figure out the best methods. We did too. This tradition of established vendors helping new vendors sets the mood for the entire market. I believe this spills over into our relationships with customers, setting the stage for all to be successful.

CHAPTER 21

WEATHER CHALLENGES

Market gardeners are at the mercy of the weather as are all farmers, not just at the market wrestling our awnings, but also managing the gardens. Perhaps it teaches patience and humility, but in the Spring, it is annoying as hell.

Illinois is known for it's bipolar weather, especially from January through May. The average last frost date is May 15 in our zone, but some years, the weather fairy doesn't mind her calendar. There has been more than one year we have rushed home on Mother's Day at dusk to get cover on tender plants.

We made the decision early on to offer lettuce blends as a featured product at the market. We do try to push the seasons as much as possible and plant early crops. At times, this requires special care to keep these tender plants viable. Imagine, if you will, two fifty-some-thing women dragging bedsheets into the garden in the dim light of the moon. Finding the moonlight too dim to keep from stumbling our way through newly sprouted lettuce and young tomato plants, we turned two cars toward the garden and used headlights as make-shift spot-lights. There was no way to hide from passersby now. We decided it was more important to save the crops than our pride.

Picture these same women tip-toeing through mud to pick a few fresh greens for supper, another event that has happened on more than one occasion. If you ever happen to drive by the Farm, be sure to go slow enough to check what may be happening. Often it is a sight to behold.

After the rush home and bedsheet in the garden incident, we dropped into our recliners and became overwrought with laughter at ourselves. We know we looked like wild women in the moonlight. I would give good money to have a video of that along with other things we do. In the midst of this we are happy. Challenges, yes, but we find joy in meeting those challenges.

CHAPTER 22

WHAT STANDS IN OUR WAY

Producing a good quality product in sufficient quantity for market is a weekly challenge. Our week starts early with predicting what produce will be ready at the end of the week. One of the summer blessings on our farm is wild blackberries and black raspberries. Donna does most of the picking as she has a higher tolerance for heat than I do. My job is to turn those berries into jam. Now I have discovered a new reason for her to do the picking.

It started as a routine morning task for Donna. A short walk out to the wild blackberry patch to gather what has become the basis of jar after jar of sweet, thick, dark jam. She didn't expect anything to go awry.

Blackberries ripen here in July. Just when the heat of summer rises along with humidity to create a natural sauna hovering over the blackberries. The wildness grows up to just over her head, so pushing through the blackberries making a path requires considerable effort and caution. Wild blackberry brambles have wicked thorns that reach out and grab the very top layer of skin and won't let go until the penance of blood has been extracted. The addition of long sleeves, hat, long pants, socks; essentially covering every inch of skin adds to the sweltering.

So there she goes walking miles in the heat in full hazmat gear to gather sweet delicious berries, in the back of her mind hoping the payoff is worth it.

Blackberry brambles are a sea of green leaves woven together with brown and green branches. Spots of dark berries dot the mass like eyes. The rhythm of gathering those dark globes takes over the watchfulness along with the sweat dripping and stinging one's eyes.

Just in the midst of mind traveling to entertain herself while picking, comes that creepy prickling up the back of her neck. Someone or something is watching.

There is no one around. It is a solitary activity. But the sense of being watched grows.

I understand and accept there are snakes on the property. I know there is a purpose for these wily creatures in nature although I am certain that a nicer, furry being could also fill that niche. It is without any embarrassment that I admit my combination of fear and hatred of these bottom dwellers in the animal kingdom. I take the story of Adam and Eve in the Garden to mean all serpents are inherently evil and should be avoided at all costs lest one be condemned straight to hell on the spot. I do understand this will not literally occur; but one can not be too careful in these matters. Despite my knowledge and acceptance I do not want to meet up with these beasts.

I have even subjected friends to vicarious trauma. On one occasion I nearly pushed my best friends off a mountain at the mere sight of a snake. In spite of my intellectual knowledge of snakes, their role in the world and knowing there are only a few poisonous ones around where we live; I maintain any snake is dangerous, even if not poisonous. Here's my stance: all snakes are dangerous because I will freak out when I see one, causing potential trauma to myself and any others nearby.

I try to tell myself there are no snakes on our property. I know this is a lie. But it is what I tell myself, even out loud when necessary. I can deal with almost anything else about living in the country, most of it I embrace. But the snakes: not at all. I know they are there. I just prefer not to see them.

Even when my brain acknowledges these are common snakes I see —water snakes, black snakes, garter snakes—they remain snakes. I know they are beneficial in the cycle of life with a job description of keeping the rodent population in check. On that front, they aren't really doing a good job, as some of our outbuildings continue to be overrun with mice. Traps actually do a better job of managing the rodent population than the snakes. But I digress.

There is an actual photo Donna's snake event I described above, but the one in my mind is much more graphic. The snake in my mind is much larger and more dangerous than the one that appeared in the brambles. My imagination has a six foot, shrewd creature with large fangs dripping poisonous saliva. In my mind, this snake even has the power of conscious thought, planning how it will grab a human and brag to it's friends back at the local snake bar over cocktails later that night.

She reached for one last big juicy berry and there it lurked. One of the brown and green stripes of branch is in fact a long body and two of those dark globes are actual eyes. A garter snake has wound itself through the berry patch to wait. Who knew garter snakes are so fond of climbing up through the brambles and waiting for lunch to appear? Patiently hanging still in the briars, slithery skin unharmed by the thorns, the snake waits and watches.

If it were me reaching within inches of that vile poison dripping monster, it would have had all the berries it wanted from now until eternity.

CHAPTER 23
EQUIPMENT CHALLENGE

This journey is not without other challenges. Sometimes the challenges are not in the form of weather or snakes but our equipment.

Scones are one of our specialties at the Farmer's Market. People come to our booth for their breakfast and often stock up for later in the week. The weekly baking has become quite a production with prepping ingredients the day before, preparing packaging and advertising flavors. Saturday finds us early to rise, laying out the utensils and firing up the ovens. It is a routine both familiar and comforting in it's sameness. The dry ingredients mix with wet, are shaped and baked to provide the quick tender treat. We have developed a production line system that allows for an almost commercial outcome in a normal household kitchen. Of course, one critical piece of equipment supports this effort: the oven.

What are scones without an oven? Nothing but a gooey wet mess of dough.

One Monday, I was baking. Nothing in particular, not for market, just baking something or other. A loud pop rang through the kitchen and the oven went silent.

A silent oven is a problem in our house. When I say silent, I am referring to not just the clicking sounds or whoosh that all ovens make. This is a convection oven, designed with a fan in the back to circulate the heated air around the oven cavity. The temperature is equal throughout the oven and food bakes faster; up to 25% faster. That is a significant time saving bonus when one is baking in a hurry. It is particularly handy with scones because that rush of heated air helps with the immediate rise, making the scones tender and thick.

But on this Monday, the pop and subsequent silence alerted me the oven was in trouble. It was virtually crying out for help, reminding me that it is a home model being used as a commercial unit. Although it is one of the higher end ovens, a Kitchen Aid, it had reached it's limit.

I made a call to the repair folks. Yes, they can have someone look at it, order a part and then come back to install said part. I described the problem again. If I was willing to take a chance it was just a heating element as my description sounded, the diagnostic visit could be eliminated. One trip and the damaged part will be installed this week. Even better. I needed that oven.

Repeated calls through the week to check on the status of my repair no doubt aggravated the repair people. I need my oven with "need" being the operative word. I'm not sure the repair people fully appreciated my level of need. Finally the call came. The part is in and the repairman is on his way.

As soon as I saw his caller ID show up at 3:00 PM on Friday, I knew it was not good. He didn't have the part on his truck and it was too far to return to the store to get it and return to my house by the end of the day.

"Really? You forgot? Didn't we just talk about this?"

My brain ranted on.

"Twelve miles is too far?"

Instead I formed more reasonable words between brain and mouth.

"How about I go get the part and get it to the house? Can you still install it today?" It is not the same crisis for the repair man who will go home to his house in two hours where his oven works. He probably won't even use his oven this weekend. Maybe I could go to his house and use his oven.

"Are you sure? Yes, I can install it if I have the part. Won't take but a few minutes." Music to my ears.

A fast twelve mile each way drive for me; a quick handoff of the part to Donna at the edge of town and an even faster installation of the heating element for him. All of the coordination paid off and the oven was once again in working order. Well, working order is a relative term. It heats more unevenly now but it does heat up. Uneven I can manage with technique.

The Saturday morning baking is a well choreographed dance. First thing after stumbling into the kitchen, even before firing up the crucial caffeine producing pot, I start the ovens. Scones require a high heat, referred to as a "quick" oven in generations past.

Between leaving dream land at 3:30 on Saturday morning and leaving the driveway in a fully loaded truck at 6:50 A.M., 216 scones of various sizes in 6 flavors move from raw ingredients to labeled packages. That's 72 scones an hour for you math geeks. Everything is timed to ensure that a quality product moves to market. There is no time for error or unexpected delays—like a lack of power.

Living in the country offers a multitude of benefits, but also comes with some risk. Not that power can't go out in town, but we seem to have an inordinate number of power outages here at the end of the co-op line.

It has happened before, just as company was coming and things were in the oven, that the power went out. The problem occurs so much that we installed a whole house generator. But we had never tested whether the generator be able to power two ovens running on high heat.

We thought the oven scare was over when we burned out an element on a Monday. A week later, the power went out briefly during baking. I wouldn't exactly term it panic, but when the ovens shut off in the middle of baking, I move to high alert.

There was only one pan of scones in the oven at the time and the next batch was still waiting for wet ingredients to be added to dry, so if the process had to be stopped, it was as good a place as any to stop. Quickly we tried to think about a fall back plan. We would simply sell whatever we had and hope the power was back on quickly. It was only a power flicker, but the ovens did not come back on.

I ran to the basement to see what was the matter. Everything in the breaker box seems fine, but I toggled the switch off and on just to be sure. Still nothing. This is definitely cramping my baking style so I take a moment to think. It has to be the breakers; every thing else is back on and working. Down to the basement again. Maybe the last attempt was the wrong breaker. I ran my finger down the list, number 21 and 23 is the oven. Toggle off and on again. Bingo, the ovens are back on and we finish in time to head to the market. Once again we have persevered.

For the rest of the season, when I hit those buttons, I made a quick mental plan just in case the power goes out in the middle of baking. We have learned that above all we must be flexible which is a good life lesson in addition to a useful mindset for market. There is an additional underlying thought of not wanting to disappoint customers.

CHAPTER 24
ATTENTION TO QUALITY

Being a small producer gives us a relationship with our product. The business model of the big box stores is to ship in produce from across the U.S. or other countries. You can find out what country of origin is stamped on the box. You can ask when it arrived at the store but that is the limit of their information. Some do try to source locally, but their concept of local is 400 miles. Ours is 10.

I understand this is their business model and place in the economy. I choose to have a closer relationship with as much of my food as possible and to share the same with friends and neighbors. Why would someone work all week and then get up early to go to the market on Saturday?

Getting up before dawn to bake scones is not something I thought I would be able to do week after week. I've always loved to bake, but I've never been a morning person. As I've visited and appreciated other bakeries I've thought about those early mornings, day after day. How do they manage their lives and get themselves up to bake so people like me could have a fresh product first thing in the morning?

I've discovered it takes passion and commitment to provide the best quality product. Almost every baked good is best when fresh. There are exceptions, but that certainly does not include scones.

We have determined our standard of excellence is to be able to tell people our scones were fresh baked that morning. Even when the customer is the first to the booth and they have just rolled out of bed, here we are to provide a treat for the consumer. Yes it is early but seeing the surprise on someone's face about the freshness of their purchase is worth rolling out of my own bed.

At the Farmer's Market, the customer comes face to face with the baker. There is no intermediary. The ones who started with basic ingredients; measured, combined, baked and packaged is standing before the customer. Feel free to ask about the exact ingredients, even though the label has a list. The baker can even identify when this particular product was made and packaged. With a bit of thought about the flavor and a brief calculation of time, I can give you a 15 minute window of when your scone came out of the oven. You won't get that at Dunkin' Donuts.

The same is true with our produce. Most is picked and packaged on Friday with a few delicate items like basil picked just before leaving for market. The grower (Donna) can tell a customer everything about their selection from seed to fruit. You can ask when the plant was started, what amendments and pest treatments have been used. You will find for our Farm that means no insecticides, no herbicides, no fungicides, no artificial 'cides of any kind are used. The soil is built from black dirt and compost. No other fertilizers than the occasional Epsom Salt treatment. It is easy to describe how the produce was picked and handled because it was done within the last 24 hours. You can ask about specific varieties, rainfall and growth tendencies of that particular plant. Almost always, you can also find out whether we like a particular variety, how the flavor compares to others and how we use it.

We have also added a couple of carefully selected growers to help provide variety in our weekly offering. These growers subscribe to the same philosophy we do regarding their produce. When we pick up produce from them, whether it be potatoes, onions, okra, pie pumpkins or sweet corn we find out what the variety is and inquire about how it was grown. These are people we know personally and can vouch for their attention to their gardens.

Try asking those questions down at your local grocery. Will the person stocking the produce be able to give a detailed answer about how the crop was grown, when it was harvested and any chemicals used during the growing season? I think not.

This attention to detail and focus on quality garners praise from our customers. The compliments about our products help spur us along and always seem to come at the right time. Some weeks are just hard. We get tired and things come up that set us back in our goals. Each time that happens, we are buoyed up by the appreciation of our customers. When we sell out week after week, it is a vote of confidence to continue what we are doing. The support of our customers gets us through the hard times.

Even though it is a lot of work and tiring, it is also energizing. We can look forward, peer into the future and see that this Farm, this business may take us places. We really may be able to support ourselves in our next careers from this venture.

CHAPTER 25

PRIDE IN PRODUCT

W e truly enjoy being able to identify when our products were produced; whether that is baked goods, wax products, or scones.

Scones are a matter of pride for me as you can surely see by now. It is important for me to provide the freshest and highest quality product possible. The dry ingredients are prepped the night before, but all of the mixing and baking is done the morning of the market. These are hand-made, small batch and hand packed.

As a creature of habit, I always make the batches in approximately the same order. This habit came in handy one morning when a particularly pinched old man came to look at our wares.

He's surely in his eighties judging by the stoop of his carriage. He shops around the market and rarely spends much, not even a word of greeting. Occasionally, he will pick up an item or two. He peruses our stand, but most often does not buy from us.

One morning, the old man stopped at our booth and picked up a small package of scones.

"When were these made?"

It was the tone that galled me just a bit. It clearly sent a message that he was looking for an excuse not to buy and justify to me why he wasn't making a purchase.

"What flavor are you holding there? Blueberry. Let's see those were the third batch out of the oven this morning, so probably around 5:15 AM today."

That answer set him back a little. He didn't expect anything quite so precise. The corner of his mouth turned up slightly. He opened his wallet and pulled out $3.00.

I rode that feeling the rest of the day. It wasn't the amount of the sale, but winning over a curmudgeon that put wind in my sails.

CHAPTER 26

TOMATOES IN MAY

The Farmer's Market opens in mid-May, just in time to have early garden produce; lettuces, radishes, possibly green onions. But people want tomatoes. I'm not sure if people don't have a good grasp on the local food and what is seasonally available, or they just want to see what you'll say.

A customer approached us one cool mid-May market, clearly looking for something in particular.

"May I help you?"

"Do you have any tomatoes?" she inquired.

"No, sorry, tomatoes won't ripen until the first of July."

She looked at me like we had just asked for the sacrifice of her first-born child to get a simple tomato.

"Does anyone else have tomatoes?"

I tried to stop my mouth from gaping open, only halfway successful. Truly, she must not have heard my first response.

"I don't think so, unless they are reselling produce from the southern states. Local tomatoes won't be available until July. Late June if we have perfect weather."

I didn't want her to think I was criticizing any other vendor if they did have tomatoes today, so I quickly continued.

"If they do have tomatoes and label where they were grown, it is perfectly legal. They just won't be locally grown."

I swear she almost hrumphed and marched away.

It isn't realistic to have home grown tomatoes in Central Illinois in May. A couple of vendors do ship in from southern states to provide this quintessential and much desired summer fruit but they fully disclose the provenance. There is no slight of hand but people are so starved for tomatoes they will stand in line for the next best thing to locally grown.

Tomatoes take good warm sunny days to ripen, plus cooperative weather to grow the plants and set blossoms. The fruit takes a while to develop and then ripen. This is not an instant process. Even the gardeners will tell you it seems to take forever to get those first juicy slicers. Just because it is a Farmer's Market doesn't mean that we will have tomatoes on any given day. The same holds true with sweet corn. There are varieties ripening earlier and earlier but there is just not enough warmth for everything to be ready at once in this area. Plus the sweet corn season is relatively short, perhaps four to six weeks to get the best and the sweetest.

Consumers have become accustomed to buying any type of fruit or vegetable at any point in the year. There are advantages to this, in terms of having a varied diet, but consumers need to understand that any time they are eating off season vegetables, there is a nutritional sacrifice. For each mile the product moves from the field it loses vital nutrients. The closer you consume your food to the actual source, the more you will benefit from that food.

Before we started as vendors at the Farmer's Market, I didn't realize how disconnected people have become from their food sources. My intent is not to be critical of our customers, but the society in which we live. It is amazing how many grow up with supermarkets and produce available year round and don't realize the seasonal nature. We expect ready access to lettuce, greens, tomatoes, peppers, and tropical fruit at any time of year. Consumers complain about the prices of these items without realizing why the cost is so high.

Part of what we do at the market is educate our consumers. We are in the middle of Illinois with a certain type of soil and growing season. As much as we have all become accustomed to vegetables year round, these are not locally grown or sourced. I too buy fruits and vegetables that are either not native to Central Illinois or when my home preserved stock runs out. My criticism is aimed at the lack of knowledge exhibited about natural food. Buy whatever you wish but do so with a conscious awareness. Some season extending does occur, but we will never have garden ripe tomatoes at the beginning of the market season.

CHAPTER 27

TOMATO DISCUSSIONS

W here two or more gardeners are gathered together you will
hear a lot of conversation about plants. They will cover varieties, growth characteristics and production. Naturally the Farmer's
Market is full of gardeners, so Saturday morning conversations often
revolve around plants.

Tomatoes are a perfect example. Most of the vendors at our
Farmer's Market grow heirloom varieties. It is a point of pride to have
either the earliest tomato, the best looking or the tastiest. Each vendor
has their favorite variety or size of tomato. We like to be able to share
with customers information about the flavor profile and recommended
use of specific tomato varieties. We get into the finer details of what
each variety is known for and how to maximize use. At the end of
these conversations it is not uncommon to have an exchange of fruit.
You might think the purpose is simply to take and eat. However, often
the goal is to harvest the seed for planting next year. You might think
this just helps the competition. Perhaps it does. But more so, it builds
relationships which are more valuable in the long run. A community
has developed among the gardeners.

These conversations about vegetable varieties make a connection
with vendors but also with customers. Customers love to hear about

when the produce was harvested, how it's been treated or what we recommend in terms of flavor. We try to describe potential uses for new varieties. If we don't have something available we refer to another vendor who does have what the customer needs. The other vendors do the same, referring to us when possible.

CHAPTER 28
DEVELOPING PRODUCTS

One of the concerns we had early on, especially the very first day, was if everyone else at the market had the same things we did. Sure enough, we hauled out our items and people next to us had the same things. There is a honey vendor with a wider variety and a nice looking display. There were people selling plants, big full garden plants. There were baked goods.

But we always have something the others don't. We have us. We have the draw of our unique name that makes people stop and ask what we do and who we are. We have cat toys. We engage people with our own personalities.

From the beginning we have exceeded our own expectations. We didn't know how this would go for us but it is going quite well actually. We sell our produce and our baked goods, usually selling out every week. We continue to have perennial items; lip balm, skin balms and cat toys we sell a few of every week.

Developing the cat toy idea was a classic example of how we work together.

"We need to think of more products."

It's a constant refrain. If one of us doesn't start the conversation, the other one will.

"Something for cats. Catnip toys, maybe."

Since we are Five Feline Farm, we really must provide some type of cat product.

It was a plausible idea. But could we really find the time and skill to create these? Cats are known to be finicky; can we even get a home-made toy past their inherent disdain for all things human made? Time to experiment.

Now, I have very little skill with a sewing machine. I can run a basic straight line and I understand the simplest part of running the dang thing.

We found an idea that works well for us. It is a simple pattern, an oval or sometimes a square shape. We cut up old material from Grandma's scrap pile, old chef pants and even some worn out jammie pants. The first ones were even packed with stuffing from an old pillow. The catnip is grown on the Farm, dried, then mixed with the stuffing material. These cat toys are a perfect fit for us since it involves recycling as many of the materials as possible and the fact it can be done in several steps. This helps us do these in stages which works well with our schedules.

It's the funniest thing. Random scraps of material, poorly sewn together and filled with more scraps plus our own catnip. Maybe it's the low price or the impulse buy factor, but we can barely keep up with demand for these little toys. Perhaps it is that they are cat tested and cat approved.

There is also the joy of watching people get interested in these toys.

"I don't have a cat, but my sister does." Substitute sister with friend, aunt, grandma, cousin.

"I'm going there next week. She will love it if I bring Sheba a toy."

And when they return, we get feedback.

"She loved the little toy. I'm going to buy two more for my other sister's cats."

On it goes, the gift of a simple toy.

CHAPTER 29

DEVELOPING RELATIONSHIPS

This particular market, as I suspect is true with most Farmer's Markets, is set up so vendors are in the same location week after week. It is good for both the vendor and the customer. Vendors come in before the market opens, know exactly where to pull in and begin to set up. We have our system of unloading and setting up down to a science which leaves us a bit of time before the first rush to talk with our neighbors.

We share typical farmer talk about the weather, if it will rain this week, what is coming up next in the garden, or how a particular variety is faring this year. We discuss who might be there the next week and what they will be bringing. Tidbits are shared about other markets attended and what those look like compared to this one. It is a bit gossipy but also breeds a sociability and community. We can join in this talk of weather and vegetables.

"Did you get any rain this week?"

A good farmer on any scale can talk about the rain.

"We had a couple of inches, but it came down so hard it didn't do us much good."

Our neighbor nods knowingly.

Neither of us shared significant history or deep emotional wounds, but we each felt comfortable in the banter. This carried on for several Saturdays in a row.

One week, without warning, we pulled in to find a new vendor in our place. We were separated from our comfortable neighbor by someone who hadn't been there the first few weeks. This new vendor was obviously someone who was known to others, although not to us. We felt violated and pushed to the side by this interloper even though it wasn't their fault. They came in and started to set up where they were shown to go. They were in our spot and it felt awkward. It's an interesting feeling to be moved a mere ten feet out of our new comfort zone and be so disjointed. What claim did we have to the space between the fourth and fifth yellow lines? Sometimes the agitation inside is unbecoming when faced with the truth of reality. I have no right to ownership of that space. We moved ten feet. Did I really imagine no one would see us in that remote area of the parking lot? My emotions boggle my own mind at times.

We scooted down and settled in. A bit off our game to start being out of sorts and feeling like the newcomers were trying to take our place. Even worse, these newcomers were old hands at this market game giving the appearance that even though this was their first arrival of the season, they were the veterans. I shrank back into myself a bit acknowledging I was still a little green at this vendor thing. Maybe I would hide in the lettuce.

The newcomers are very nice. They even bought some things from us. Once I accepted this was not actually my turf but a shared place I discovered the newcomers were quite supportive and encouraging.

The week after that we were back to our regular arrangement. I breathed a sigh and felt much better. We were next to our usual friend and could visit freely again. The world had righted itself.

Vendor life settled in again with a comfortable rhythm of early mornings and summer heat. We somehow belong to this random group of souls gathering on black asphalt over tomatoes.

CHAPTER 30
LEARNING THROUGH OBSERVATION

It doesn't always have to be direct interaction to learn from others. Yes, there have been times we have swallowed our pride and asked for advice. But we've also found you can just figure out a lot by watching others.

We had the great fortune of being placed next to a veteran market vendor our first season. They had an established group of customers, who would shop with them no matter what they have and no matter what they are offering or is available from other vendors. We didn't have quite so many customers that first year, so it was a good time to observe. We watched and learned their sales techniques. This is not a high pressure sales venue. In fact, hawking is strictly forbidden. The atmosphere is designed to be welcoming and friendly, not obnoxious. Marketing is done in subtle ways.

They invited customers in to their tent. They explained details about their products.

She says "That will be just $3.00" or whatever the amount is.

The key word is "just". She is making a subtle statement in her sale, establishing that it is a smaller amount than it could have been and reinforcing that the customer is getting a quality product for a great price.

This helped me immensely in an area where I feel the least confident. I hate to charge for things; I don't know if I'm asking too much, but I do want to make money.

I don't think I have incorporated this into my own practice consistently but I like the way it sounds. I keep practicing.

CHAPTER 31

CONTINUALLY MAKING NEW FRIENDS

F inding new relationships has been one of the unexpected bonuses in becoming a vendor at the Farmer's Market. We've met neighbors and made new friends. We take advantage of times when the market is slow and accept the opportunity to talk instead of staying to ourselves. The realization of how much we would miss these connections during the off-season was apparent during the last market of our first season.

The weather forecast was sketchy. It was the first weekend of October. In Illinois, that can mean anything from scorching heat to blizzard conditions. This particular Saturday was somewhere in between.

I didn't blame the customers or the vendors for not wanting to come out in nasty weather. Mother Nature was certainly in a grumpy mood, wearing her grayest cloak to keep her from the chill in the air. To top it off, she must have had a slight virus since she kept dripping on us.

The market manager offered the building canopy to the few brave vendors. We set up under the bit of protection and savored not wrestling with our awnings all morning.

There were four of us. Not four people, but four booths. The traffic was slow and we had an opportunity to talk to some of the vendors that weren't typically close by in a regular market arrangement.

The small group was a lot of fun. We talked about the weather and our plans for the winter. A couple were headed south for the winter while we planned to stay and persevere with whatever the aforementioned Mother Nature had planned.

Here it was the end of the season and we made more friends.

CHAPTER 32

NEW MARKET FLOW

S ometimes it is the little things that really make a difference. We have experimented with different arrangements of our tables and how our products are displayed. One year found a change in the way the entire market was laid out.

For the first two years we were arranged in the same order more or less and on one side of the parking lot. We really started to depend on the vendors on either side of us. We looked for them when it was time to pull in to find our space. Picture a large open parking lot. It is a bit of a guessing game to find your correct location from week to week.

So not only did we depend on these others for our location but also for conversation. We really got to know each other during those hours on Saturday mornings. If either of us were going to miss a market week we let each other know so no one worried. We had established a connection deep enough to take note of the other's well-being.

After a couple of years the market manager changed the market and set up a bit different traffic flow. The new arrangement really made a difference in terms of the feel of the market. It now felt more like a city-style pedestrian market with vendor booths aligned around a central walkway. We found we had a new vendor neighbor. Once again we had to learn new relationships and to make new connections.

It was a funny feeling to miss our old neighbors even though we could see them across the way. We could still go over and talk to them but it was different. During those slow business times, you can visit with your neighbors, but there is limited time to walk all around the market. You just don't want to leave your booth unattended long enough to have a deep conversation with someone across the market. What if you get a customer? Even when our relationships among vendors changed, the relationship with customers and the atmosphere of the new market arrangement was a bonus.

There truly is room for everyone at this market.

CHAPTER 33

EXPANSION

Not only is there room for everyone but we have room for improvement and we always try to up our game.

We work on our presentation of items each and every week. Improved signage appears or prices change to meet market demand. When possible, we add additional products to enhance our product line. Things like more wax based products and more baked goods and jams from the kitchen. Our set up has expanded to two awnings and multiple tables covered with as much product choice as we can muster.

We are expanding our social media efforts. Facebook has it's own issues but has shown promise in getting our name known. We would rather have our following grow organically than pursue high numbers. We are on Twitter, which is a learning curve and somewhat different than our Facebook efforts. Instagram has gathered a nice following of those who enjoy the photo documentation of Farm growth. We may not gain a hoard of customers through some of these channels but each has a place.

PART III
TOGETHER AND BELONGING

CHAPTER 34
MEETING CUSTOMER REQUESTS

We have found part of the charm of a Farmer's Market is the connection between the vendor and customers. Our personal mission is to provide not only quality products but an excellent standard of customer service. In doing so, we have had to change our initial stance on ordering ahead for certain items.

We have had many special requests to save things back for people. It took input from others though to see the benefit in honoring these requests, especially with scones. These sell fast on Saturday morning and it was not uncommon for regular customers to miss out on their favorites.

Our operation is a small, handmade, high quality control system. We do small batch in everything from lettuces to special variety tomatoes to our baked goods. This allows us to maintain the highest quality product possible. We have very high standards with a limited supply. We have had a lot of disappointed customers who arrive only an hour or two after the market opens to discover they missed what they were hoping to find. Then we began receiving the inevitable requests to hold something back.

Now we found ourselves in a predicament. We don't want to disappoint anyone, but we also do not want to compromise our standards of product. What to do?

We found the answer in two places. First was at an exclusive restaurant near us. This one of a kind place only offers meals on Thursday through Saturday and by reservation only. During one of our trips there, we asked about their desserts. We've noticed their Thousand Leaves dessert, a flaky pastry layered with vanilla cream is a customer favorite and wondered if it would be rude to ask for one to be held back for us. Our disappointment is evident when they run out. The owner offered her perspective.

"The Chef loves when someone reserves a dessert when they make their reservation. It helps him plan for the upcoming week and can ensure enough is available for all."

We hadn't thought about that approach.

The second question that solidified our change in policy was from a friend.

"Have you ever been burned by someone who asked you to hold an order?"

"No."

In fact we haven't. Anyone who has ever asked us to pre-bag their order has always shown up and always paid for their order.

"It's a guaranteed sale."

Well indeed it is.

Ordering ahead or sending a message to save a special favorite has alleviated difficulties for both us and the customers. We can make extra if time allows; the customer is happy and satisfied, plus we are guaranteed a sale. That is much better than having a lot of product left at the end of the market, particularly perishable items. I still feel bad when we sell out, but there is only so much time on Saturday morning.

Now we prepare ahead and have a plan to hold certain orders. It's a win-win for us and the customer. In altering our policy we find we have gained additional customers who are building relationships with us through social media and special orders.

CHAPTER 35

MUSIC

Each week there is music playing at the market; occasionally it is a local radio station but often it is live music. All types of music are welcome and a variety of groups have played. My favorites have been the acoustic groups offering coffee house types of music. This is a nice feature of the market and creates a relaxed atmosphere inviting people to linger.

One Saturday, a group of local musicians played using a Karaoke style arrangement. The selections were mostly older tunes, ones my grandparents or maybe parents would have enjoyed. Even though it is not my preferred style of music, many of the customers appeared to enjoy it. I mostly tune it out. I'm occasionally embarrassed when it's obvious I know all the words to a Roger Miller song. I carry on our commerce, waiting on customers, helping with product selections and explaining the benefits of one balm over another.

As I was waiting on a customer, I heard the melody of a familiar tune, "I'll Fly Away". This old hymn is familiar to so many, even those who likely have not been to church in years, if ever. There is a catchy repetitive lilt in the music, inviting participation. I found myself humming and then singing along absentmindedly. A quick glance around the market revealed I was not the only one who could not keep quiet. Virtually everyone, vendors and customers alike were singing along. My throat was full of my heart to recognize this shared experience. We were all joined as one in that moment, connected by a hymn from the early 1900's that spans events from funerals to bluegrass jams to now our Farmer's Market. For me it is a moment, a memory frozen in time, of belonging to a larger group, a community.

CHAPTER 36
BECOMING A REGULAR

We didn't really know who our customers would be at the market. Each week the crowd has been a little bit different. There are the regulars who attend almost every week and shop the same vendors. There are occasional shoppers who come often enough to be familiar but not to develop a conversational relationship week to week. The message goes out through social media we are there and what we are selling. Some folks come specifically for something we have advertised. That is a wonderful feeling.

We look for our regular customers and worry about them when they miss a week. They comment about missing us when we have a week off. It is good to be missed.

Despite the ever changing customer base, each week we make a new connection or someone we know from outside the market will stop in to chat or buy. We enjoy the conversation and connections even when someone isn't there to buy, but only to share a story or bit of information. We've been given recipes, instructions, family history, photographs and gifts. It is not uncommon for weeks to go by before we learn someone's name, but still there is a relationship built. A relationship built on a shared experience of attending the Farmer's Market.

CHAPTER 37

WE BELONG

There has been an overwhelming sense of community in this adventure. It started with the vendors and became a connection to our customers. We went into the first Farmer's Market knowing so very little about what we were doing. It started as a way to plan for the future and have another source of income plus a market for our excess.

Our participation in this market has become so much more. We have made friends. We have joined our community. Our community has accepted us as willing participants in the arena we call the Farmer's Market.

Farmer's Markets in this part of the country have historically been in the larger cities or in the form of roadside stands. Now the small intimate markets are starting to grow. Our market is of this variety. It is the people who grow or produce the goods that set up a stand and peddle their wares week after week. The vendors know their product and can describe it in detail. These are not hired staff, paid to sell what others have bought or grown or made. It is different than a grocery.

The sense of community at the 18th Street Farmer's Market is palpable. It is a coming together of those who produce and those who consume. Conversations will continue to occur over which type of tomato each prefers. Vendors who may not grow a particular vegetable make it a habit to tell customers when the vendor who does sell that item will be back. We all willing share when the trailer full of sweet corn will arrive.

We all belong here. This mixed group of vendors and customers. Different backgrounds and philosophies, religions and ethnicities, even in such a small town. This is not just a story of us or the market vendors. It is also the story of those who come to the market to shop week after week. Those who meet up with old friends, people they haven't seen in a while then stand and talk in the middle of the market. We overhear snippets of their conversations.

"I haven't seen you in forever, how have you been?"

"I come to the market just to see people and visit."

Several of our customers seem to just come and talk to us. These relationships have developed organically through times at the market we stand huddled together under our awning during an unexpected downpour. Or when we discover by chance that we have acquaintances in common. Often it is just that we met over the market table, sharing stories of our week past, interests and plans for the future.

We are now in the Senior Class, ready for Prom. We no longer have the fear of the unknown or worries of competition. No questions of who will have a prettier dress or if we have the same dress, metaphorically speaking. We know it is ok. No matter what comes our way, we have built our own little niche carved from the asphalt dance floor.

Our guiding principle has been to take things one step at a time and just keep taking the next step as we figure out what this business is to become. We have an end result in mind. A nice Farm where different areas are featured so that others can come and enjoy what we have built. But it is more than that. A place to work hard and rest. A place that gives us time and room to grow. A place that provides for us.

We don't know exactly where we are headed yet, but are confident time will reveal the path. Without a doubt we are determined to follow this dream. We have discovered our place in this community and it fits.

EPILOGUE

Our tribe is now following us. We have built relationships that continue to be nurtured. As we move forward in our business plan, we opened a small store at the Farm named The Farm Fresh Mercantile. It is a little different venue than the Farmer's Market and gives us an outlet for our wares outside of the Farmer's Market days. We can be open through the winter when we choose.

But the community we developed at the Farmer's Market, week after week for a few hours at a time, building relationships and a following; they are our tribe. That group now seeks us out. We find they want to engage in conversation, they ask about products, they inquire about our lives and we ask about theirs.

It is a sense of belonging. We have come full circle.

AFTERWORD

Once again, the alarm goes off at 3:30 AM on Saturday and I roll out of bed. Anyone who knows me understands this is special. I don't like to get up in the morning and I don't wake easily. Waking up in the middle of the night, with everything dark is an event. My passion to bake is as strong as coffee.

It took a few weeks to get the system down pat, but in just over two hours, we crank out 216 scones. The first batch of scones is in the oven around 3:50 AM. We make 32 at a time, thankfully we have double wall ovens or it would not be possible to manage. Each of us has our routine. It is also a quiet time for us to talk. We chat about the weather, the business and what customers we will see. The repetitive nature of the work allows our minds the freedom to think and discuss.

It has been surprising how much I enjoy those early Saturday mornings. It feels almost magical to be up and active during the wee hours of the morning. The house is quiet except for the clanking of the pastry cutter against the stainless steel bowl. The rhythm of the baking soothes my soul and I find that this is good for me. Unlike the rest of my world, baking is predictable. When you add an acidic liquid (buttermilk) to a leavening agent (baking powder and baking soda), it will rise. Eggs tenderize as well as add body and flavor. If you do the same things over and over, it works the same.

It looks like an assembly line in the kitchen on those early Saturday mornings. While I start the baking, Donna tends to the cat needs, then washes up to help package. The timing works perfectly. As one batch cools, the next one bakes. Just as one batch is ready to come out of the oven, the preceding one is ready for packaging.

By 6:15 AM, 216 scones are packaged and added to the produce load for the trip to town.

We head to the market.

ACKNOWLEDGMENTS

DONNA—This book, or any of my writing would not be possible without your daily support. Thank you for taking on extra chores so I can write.

MARTHA and CHERYL—Board members, readers, editors and friends. Thank you.

SUSAN—Editor, commentator, friend. Thank you.

STEVE—manager of an awesome market.

18TH STREET MARKET VENDORS—it's a pleasure standing beside you rain or shine.

OUR MARKET CUSTOMERS—it is impossible to list each of you by name, but without you, there would be no market.

ABOUT THE AUTHOR

Julia Miller is a social worker by day, author and blogger in the gaps. Her personal Twitter profile says it all, "Writer, amateur chef, modern homesteader, social worker and thinker of thoughts. I don't do plumbing."

This is Julia's second book.

ALSO BY JULIA MILLER

<u>Simply Delicious</u>

Made in the USA
Monee, IL
22 October 2023

45010807R00073